Gladnesse of the Best

The George Herbert Festival 2014

Edited by Rosie Clay

Copy no. 261   of 500

Published by the **Friends of St Andrew's, Bemerton**

Orders
friends@georgeherbert.org.uk

ISBN 978-0 9930974-0-9

Printed 2014

Copyright © Friends of St Andrew's, Bemerton

Edited by Rosie Clay, Copywriter and Editor, 83 Lower Road,
Lower Bemerton, Salisbury SP2 9NH.

Photography by Jeremy Court, Mark Cooper and Tony Oliver,
Salisbury Camera Club, unless otherwise credited.

Designed by Marketing at the Mill, Blount House,
Hall Court, Hall Park Way, Town Centre, Telford TF3 4NQ.

Printed by Baskerville Press, 24 Norton Enterprise Park,
Whittle Road, Churchfields, Salisbury SP2 7YS.

Contents

Acknowledgements

The Committee of The George Herbert Festival 2014 wishes to acknowledge with much gratitude support received from the following:

Salisbury Playhouse
Sarum College
The Trustees of Wilton House
Salisbury Cathedral
Bemerton Parish
Wilton Parish
Salisbury Camera Club
Rosie Clay

Financial support from the following was also much appreciated:

Trinity College, Cambridge
The Sarum St Michael Educational Charity
together with goodwill contributions from 23 individual benefactors

The sun shone. The crowds came. The George Herbert Festival in July 2014 was an unforgettably rich experience.

Contributors gave generously of their skills and insights. Hosts gave generously of their homes and gardens. And planners gave generously of their time and energy.

It was as if being around the poetry and life of George Herbert for a few days brought out the best of us all, and created an atmosphere of ease, happiness and deep satisfaction.

To Dr Rowan Williams, Sarum College, Salisbury Playhouse, Wilton House, Bemerton and Wilton churches, Salisbury Cathedral, all who contributed and all who came, our heartfelt thanks and appreciation.

Gladnesse and gratefulnesse abound.

Judy Rees
Festival Chairman

The first impression I had of this lovely celebration was the sheer number of people for whom Herbert mattered sufficiently to give up significant time and energy to absorb the quite formidable range of events.

So many people recognise very clearly that Herbert is not, after all, a quaint and picturesque figure from a distant age: he is a demanding and subtle poet, an analyst of difficult corners of the human heart, someone who does what good poets always do – make you at once uncomfortable and enthralled as language itself is opened up to new depths. For men and women of faith, Herbert's poetry continues to show that belief does not reduce the range or smooth out the contours of difficult experience, but tests itself again and again. And the extraordinary music and sweetness of which Herbert is capable becomes all the more compelling when we grasp how hard-won it is. John Drury's outstanding biography has put Herbert on the map in new ways by showing with such sensitivity and erudition just how this is achieved, and it was a special grace to have John present at the event.

But I also treasure the morning spent with students from Bishop Wordsworth's School and South Wilts Grammar School for Girls reading some of the poems. Quite a few teachers or schools might have decided that a seventeenth-century cleric was simply beyond the mental and emotional horizons of twenty-first century teenagers: all the more credit to the staff of these schools for resisting any such premature conclusion. I found the insights offered by the students and the work they produced in response to Herbert both fresh and mature. He had unmistakeably spoken to them and even moved them. There could have been no more powerful an affirmation for me of the worthwhileness of the event and all the devoted work that went into its planning and direction. Herbert stood revealed as what those who love him have always believed – a writer always capable of surprise, a writer who grows in stature as the reader grows in understanding. A poet for adults, who is also astoundingly simple and unvarnished; speaking out of an age of bitter conflict and confusion with a clear, resilient voice affirming that the world's depths are still inviting, still filled with unimagined grace.

Rowan Williams

George Herbert (1593-1663)

Nearly 400 years have passed since George Herbert lived in and ministered to the parish of Fugglestone-cum-Bemerton, and over that time people's awareness of him and his works has risen and fallen.

In the seventeenth century his verse was in huge demand, with no less than 13 editions of his poetry volume *The Temple* being printed between 1633 and 1709, but in the eighteenth century he was scarcely visible. Rediscovered in the 1830s, he became a religious literary beacon for the Victorians only to fade again for much of the first half of the twentieth century.

Picture courtesy of Houghton Library, Harvard University

It took the publication in the 1940s of Canon Hutchinson's magisterial collection of Herbert's works to bring him to public attention once again, and since then he has been studied and analysed as never before, especially in the USA. Perhaps only now is it possible to appreciate the enduring depth and relevance of his life and work, and its attraction both to those of many shades of religious belief and to those of no faith at all.

And yet it is for just a handful of hymn settings of his verse that Herbert is best known, and there will be many to whom his name is entirely unfamiliar. To Anglicans, who annually devote 27th February to his commemoration, he has long been seen as the archetypal country parish priest, but anyone who has read and admired his poetry soon appreciates why he deserves to be remembered chiefly for the power and skill of his devotional verse.

Born into a notable Welsh family in Montgomery and kinsman of the powerful Earls of Pembroke, he lost his father at the age of three and was raised by his mother Magdalen, a patron of John Donne. He was educated at Westminster School and Trinity College Cambridge, where he was an academic high-flier who at the age of 26 was elected Public Orator of the University. In 1624 he was briefly an MP. But in 1627 he disappeared from public view and little is known of the intervening three years before his ordination as priest of his little parish in the shadow of Salisbury Cathedral

It remains a matter of conjecture why such a well-born and talented man, with all the advantages of family connections and a prestigious academic appointment, should end his brief life in the relative obscurity of a country rectory. But of the importance of his legacy there can be no doubt, and he is now rightly seen as one of the shining stars in our literary firmament and a significant figure in our nation's history.

'A verse may finde him, who a sermon flies'

'Why 2014?' was the question we were asked most frequently both before and during the Festival. On the face of it, it was a strange choice given that George Herbert lived from 1593 to 1633. The answer was, quite simply, because the next centenary year was not until 2033 and that could be too late for many of us! We might have done it sooner, but we were also very keen to involve Dr Rowan Williams, a lover of Herbert's verse and a published poet, and we needed to identify a time when he was able to join us.

Once we had secured our principal contributor, we were able to approach others whom we knew could be relied upon to provide a wide variety of knowledgeable and interesting approaches to Herbert's life and work. We drew a few blanks, but for the most part the responses were enthusiastic and we were able to put together an interesting and attractive programme remarkably quickly.

We felt it was important that Festival venues should embrace Salisbury and Wilton as well as Bemerton. Fortunately we had a good relationship with Sarum College in the Cathedral Close, which readily agreed to provide us with a focal point. However, for our keynote events we anticipated audiences of at least 200 so we needed to look elsewhere. Luckily we discovered that the Salisbury Playhouse main house would be 'dark' at the time of the Festival and was available for hire. Taking this option turned out to be one of our happiest decisions.

As far as Wilton was concerned, our aim was clear. Herbert's association with Wilton House through his kinsfolk, the Earls of Pembroke, had been duly recognised and valued over the centuries but sadly in recent years the link had suffered a decline. The Festival provided an ideal opportunity to re-establish it and so we were delighted when, through the good offices of the Wilton Rector, the Wilton House Trustees offered us the use of the splendid Double Cube Room. This, together with the parish churches at Fugglestone and Bemerton, provided us with the spread of venues we were seeking.

The choice of Salisbury Playhouse produced a huge bonus: their box office was prepared to undertake booking and ticketing for the entire Festival. The small fee involved was money well spent, and we were relieved of a significant administrative burden. The whole process went remarkable smoothly and any minor problems that arose were speedily resolved.

Financially, our aim was just to break even. As the Festival was a new venture, there was no history to guide us about how many people might want to attend, so much of our budgeting rested on assumptions. It quickly became clear that some financial support would be prudent, and we were delighted to receive a grant from Trinity College Cambridge, Herbert's *alma mater*. In addition, a number of local residents responded generously to a fundraising initiative. This underpinning gave us the reassurance we needed.

One of our principal aims was to make the Festival accessible to all. We opted not to charge for many of the events, relying instead on retiring collections, and for the rest, where it was clear that we would have to charge, we set ticket prices as low as we could. In this way we hoped to bring in people knowing little or nothing about Herbert as well as his aficionados.

We built our programme around three evening keynote events – the talk by Rowan Williams on the Thursday, the poets' symposium on the Friday when he was joined by Gillian Clarke and Andrew Motion, and the words and music concert with the Farrant Singers on the Saturday. In the daytime, we planned concurrent events so that those attending the Festival could be offered a choice of activities and venues.

The programme consisted mainly of talks and presentations, but we were also able to include three special activities. First, we arranged a series of small poetry discussion groups; in the main, these were hosted by local residents in their own homes. Second, we programmed drop-in sessions in Herbert's two original parish churches, enabling visitors to read aloud poems of their own choosing in these evocative spaces. Third, we organised guided walks to Bemerton from both Salisbury and Wilton, tracing Herbert's footsteps. All three activities were much enjoyed by those who took part.

We were keen to involve young people in the Festival, and teenagers read poems for us at each of the Salisbury Playhouse events. Local junior schools took part in a competition based on George Herbert.

On the Friday morning, senior pupils from local grammar schools took part in a special event at Bishop Wordsworth's School, led by Rowan Williams; they could not have had a better introduction to Herbert's verse.

There was also a spiritual dimension to the programme, with Herbert-themed services each day in Salisbury Cathedral and a special Festival Eucharist on the Sunday morning, at which the preacher was Canon Mark Oakley, the Chancellor of St Paul's Cathedral. On the Friday at St Andrew's Church, following an early morning communion service, a new stone plaque in the porch was blessed by Rowan Williams.

All events were well attended, and in addition to local participants the Festival attracted many visitors from further afield, including some from overseas. In total, we issued well over 2000 tickets. We were blessed with warm, sunny weather throughout, which added to the celebratory atmosphere and allowed everyone to enjoy to the full the various outdoor events, not least the opening garden party hosted by Bishop Nicholas and Helen Holtam.

In the pages that follow you will find summaries and commentary on many of the events, which we hope will serve as a pleasant souvenir for those who attended, and will give other readers a flavour of what we believe was a fitting and timely celebration of the life and works of a man whose light is still shining brightly after almost four hundred years.

Peter Webster
Festival Co-Chairman

Why Herbert Matters

Rowan Williams

Thursday, 10th July

Salisbury Playhouse

Dr Rowan Williams took up his appointment as Master of Magdalene College, Cambridge in 2013 following ten years as Archbishop of Canterbury and three as Archbishop of Wales. Acknowledged internationally as an outstanding theological writer, scholar and teacher, he is also a published poet with an abiding interest in the life and works of George Herbert.

Following an introduction by Nicholas Holtam, Bishop of Salisbury, Rowan explained to an audience of over 450 why Herbert matters to us today. This proved to be one of the most talked-about events of the Festival, and for this reason, we include here a summary of its content. The session was prefaced by readings of 'The Elixir', 'Deniall' and 'Peace' by Alice Wordsworth, Nigel Wingate and Sonia Woolley respectively.

A good poet, a good priest, a good man

Rowan opened his talk with the statement 'Herbert matters because he was a good poet, a good priest and a good man'. He continued by exploring each of these aspects.

The good priest – in his book *The Country Parson*, Herbert writes about what is expected of clergy in communities. He writes about the Church offering a place where, then as now, people can be cared for and where people's most passionate feelings can be based.

The good man – goodness was not something that Herbert found easy: he was short-tempered, and he understood that

Top - *Bishop Holtam introduces Rowan Williams to the Salisbury Playhouse audience*

Above - *Nigel Wingate reads Herbert's poem 'Deniall' before Rowan Williams's talk*

'The most memorable experience of the Festival for me was the full and varied contribution made by the former Archbishop of Canterbury, Dr Rowan Williams: poet, theologian, public intellectual and reader of Herbert. On the first evening I heard him give a masterly presentation on "Why Herbert Matters" – and indeed he does.'

goodness came out of paying prices, that it was hard won. For him, being good was about being very specific, and he lived out goodness in a way that reminds us that goodness costs.

The good poet – Herbert was, of course, a metaphysical poet. Yet his imagery and his language speak of the everyday with a directness and simplicity that render the most complex ideas accessible and understandable.

When you think with imagery, the imagery leads you: you let the language tell you things. In 'The Agonie' Herbert uses metaphor to illustrate sin. In the words 'Sinne is that presse…', 'presse' both describes a metaphorical wine press and the literal pressure brought by sin. The final verse continues the wine metaphor, referring to the Eucharist and reminding us that love costs God, and intoxicates us.

Also notable in 'The Agonie' is the use of epigrammatic and monosyllabic words – another feature of Herbert's poetry, reminding us that he achieves what he achieves in unusual ways.

'Redemption' begins with a prosaic, conversational tone, a style with which Herbert often starts his poems. As he develops his metaphor, the language thins out into hard consonants and monosyllables, emphasising the place to which Herbert has taken his reader.

'Rowan's talk was sensational. It was wonderful to hear his personal response to the poetry. The structure was architectural, seamless. He showed such a wide range of learning.'

Herbert's technique tells us we know more than we realise, that we say more than we know. The endings of his poems are significant – frequently abrupt or monosyllabic. Within the poems, he suspends or turns the reader's expectation, as in 'Jordan (1)'. In 'Dialogue' the poet (the soul) is interrupted. The conversational, monosyllabic opening of 'The Collar' creates surprise. In 'Grief', Herbert reaches for all the clichés, yet only the last line says what can be said; the rest of the poem speaks of what cannot be said.

Above
*Rowan Williams
delivers his talk*

11

Rowan Williams

Thursday, 10th July

Salisbury Playhouse

'He chose to speak with such simplicity, humility and grace. And that communicated to everybody. The buzz and the excitement! Afterwards everyone was so delighted.'

Faith and poetry

Herbert creates a space where the presence of holiness does not seem false, speaking up to a point, then stopping. His use of paradox and extravagance of language has force both in relation to poetry of faith but it is also effective where other kinds of words will not work. His poetry takes you to a place where you don't quite know what you're saying or what to say next. Loving God leads to a sort of paralysis. 'Affliction' for instance shows that loving God is not easy; it is a savage poem of protest, a prayer of desperation and trust, all at once.

Herbert's poems speak of what belief in God is and what it is not. They demonstrate that faith is there to be tested. Implicit in his work is an act of profound trust, akin to driving a car very fast towards a cliff edge and applying the brakes at the last minute. Knowing that what is not false is where God is, where love is, it becomes possible to live with human frailty.

Conclusion

Rowan said that he had fallen in love with Herbert's poetry at the age of 16, and saw no reason now to revise his view. Herbert matters because he cares about language itself and because:

- He lets the unaccepted and the difficult work on your mind.

- His poetry teaches us to beware of false simplicities in language and to be intrigued by its difficulties.

- He takes us to a place where religious language might begin to make sense.

- Faith takes us to a place where no adequate words will cater for it, yet Herbert demystifies and demythologises some kinds of religious talk.

Faith is difficult. In his verse, Herbert asks us, 'Is this a place where you want to go? If so, read on'.

Following a question and answer session, Dr Williams ended by reading one of Herbert's best-known poems, 'Love (III)'.

'The opportunity to give voice to several of
Herbert's poems over these three days has been
a truly rich experience. I have always believed
that the words are best communicated orally
so the listener can really appreciate the rhythm
and complexity of feeling contained within the
verses – great to hear this view shared by the
distinguished members of the poets' symposium!'
(Sonia Woolley, reader)

Above
*Salisbury Playhouse
– a full house to hear
Rowan Williams*

Herbert's Direct Descendants

Beth Dodd

Friday, 11th July

Sarum College

Dr Beth Dodd is Academic Tutor and Director of Studies for STETS, the ordination training course based at Sarum College. She has co-edited a collection of essays on *Thomas Traherne and Seventeenth-Century Thought* for Boydell and Brewer, and is publishing a book with Ashgate entitled, *'Were all men Wise and Innocent...' The Boundless Innocence of Thomas Traherne*.

'Beth Dodd's masterly talk on the day had become "Herbert's Remains: the Legacy of Interpretation", a much more helpful title and one which alludes to that of the 1652 edition of The Country Parson. Beth drew out well how Herbert's successors interpreted and built on his oeuvre during the religious turbulence of the English Civil Wars (1642–4 and 1648–9) and the subsequent Restoration of the Monarchy (1660).'

Above
Beth Dodd
Picture courtesy of Beth Dodd

On her choice of subject, Beth commented, 'It occurred to me that the impact of Herbert's immediate legacy on the way that we read him today was huge. I wanted to uncover some of those early readings, particularly the ways in which Herbert was copied, appropriated and adapted. These help to shed light on the ideas and assumptions that have grown up around the man and the significance on his work.'

Between 1640 and 1670, an influential period in setting the patterns of interpretation, Beth identified three ways in which Herbert was taken on by his successors: imitation, allusion and translation.

Imitation

Opportunities for imitation were enhanced in the seventeenth century by the flowering of print. As a result, Herbert's poetry reached a relatively wide audience, and writers such as Richard Crashaw and Christopher Harvey openly imitated his work. In contrast to today, imitation did not carry such pejorative overtones. Rather, it was a way of appreciating someone else's work, and was indeed a virtue in itself.

Harvey's *The Synagogue* describes itself as an imitation of Herbert's *The Temple*. Beth illustrated the clear influence of the latter on the former, pointing out that while there may be an element of parody, imitation kept the original work alive.

Allusion

Using the example of Thomas Traherne (1637–74), the Royalist metaphysical poet who explored the life of the spirit through poetry, Beth showed how Herbert's legacy was perpetuated through allusion. Further, she argued that allusion was about creativity, and that it transformed the legacy.

In 'The Author to the Critical Peruser', for example, Traherne's words 'no curling metaphors that gild the sens', allude to Herbert's 'Jordan (II)' in which he describes his own poetry as 'Curling with metaphors…', suggesting that Traherne was responding to Herbert's call for simple language as a reflection of the divine.

Traherne alludes in a notebook entry on 'Grace' to Herbert's 'Affliction (I)', paraphrasing the poem's last two lines. This gives an insight into the next generation's interpretation of Herbert: in Traherne's own poem 'Affliction', Traherne adds the condition of poverty to his paraphrase.

Translation

Here Beth referred to the transference of meaning from one medium to another, specifically from poetry to music. Taking John Playford's 1671 setting of 'The Altar' as an example, she showed how Playford carried forward Herbert's intention. Playford's simple solo line, with music reinforcing the rhythm of the poetry, heightens the intense emotion of the words.

'Members of the Royal School of Church Music gave a vibrant performance of 'The Altar', a fitting finale to a session that fully reflected today's living legacy of George Herbert.'

'Music at Midnight'

John Drury

Friday, 11th July

Sarum College

Dr John Drury is Chaplain and Fellow of All Souls College, Oxford. Previous appointments include Resident Canon at Norwich Cathedral, Head of Religious Studies at Sussex University, Dean and Fellow of King's College, Cambridge and Dean of Christ Church, Oxford. His book *Music at Midnight* (Allen Lane, 2013) is a culmination of a lifetime's study of George Herbert. With kind permission, an edited version of his talk is given here.

In my teens I mistakenly let myself in for an evangelical summer camp. The continual sport and high-pressure religion were uncongenial to me. But one day we visited Salisbury Cathedral. Our guide paused at the recently installed George Herbert window and read us the poem which is at its source, 'Love-joy'.

I was captivated. I bought a copy of *The Temple*, read it avidly on the coach back and showed it to one of the camp staff. He was dismissive. Such stuff was unnecessary. One should just read the Bible. I knew right away he was wrong and Herbert was right. It was a decisive moment.

Why was I converted in this unintended, even contrary way? It was a matter of the tone of voice. The religion at the camp was shouted: aggressively sentimental and biblically authoritarian. Ugly, in short. In the cathedral, as the old man read that poem, it was quite different: feeling held in the courteous exchange of a brief but happy encounter – beautiful. And the window helped. Of an aesthetic disposition, I was fascinated by stained glass: 'colours and light, in one/ When they combine and mingle, bring/ A strong regard and awe'. Thus Herbert, as I found much later.

And now, after 60 years of reading Herbert, I can be clear about how 'Love-joy' works and affects. In its eight pentameter lines with their easy, modest diction it combines form and feeling perfectly. The rhyme-scheme is quite tight: a b a c b c d d. The final d is a sort of d+, 'Christ' being stronger in sound and significance than 'miss'd'. But within that net, the metre is loose and flowing, enjambments gliding over the line breaks. Then there is that wonderfully confiding and disarming aside at the centre of it all: 'I, who am never loth/ To spend my judgement, said…'.

And it helps to know Herbert's sources: the priest's bidding at the Holy Communion service; and the parable of the vine in Herbert's Bible at John 15. 'Love-joy' is a poem about nearly missing the point, but with a little help from a friend ('Sir, you have not miss'd'), not: a commonplace, such as true mystics love.

And now I have written a book about Herbert, his life and poetry. Certainly for Herbert, they belonged together. He was, in his own words as related by Walton, making 'picture[s] of the many spiritual conflicts that have passed betwixt God and my soul'. The poems are a way of objectifying his intense subjectivity, putting it out there and ordering it, getting at the truth of it and making it 'something understood'. Experience (then eliding into 'experiment'), not dogma, was primary. This puts Herbert among the pioneers of the proto-, or early, enlightenment. And the point of art of any kind, I had long believed, is that the realities which confront us are taken on by someone skilled and understanding, tested and presented to us re-objectified – the 're' denoting the artist's own added human value.

'Affliction(I)' is for Herbert an unusually large-scale 'picture' of 'spiritual conflict'. He is questioning God, the managing director of his life. His poetry, as he wrote in 'The Quidditie' was 'that which while I use/ I am with thee'. Here the rendezvous is adversarial. Notice the verbs he imputes to the deity: 'entice', 'betray', 'took'st away', 'throwest'. Notice above all the superbly tough ending: both contestants must agree to love without dissimulation as the *unum necessarium*, be-all and end-all.

A little deeper digging in Herbert's biography shows where and when he wrote it. He would have liked to be a metropolitan man but was trapped in academe. In 1620 he had become Cambridge's University Orator, an office for which he had lobbied frantically and recklessly, but despite his masterful Latin Oration in 1623 against war with Spain, which Cambridge loved, 'Affliction (II)' shows that he hated it all. The great prize of Oratorship was dust and ashes. He gradually alienated himself from it and Cambridge, resigning a few years later.

This was a crisis of identity, eventually solved when Herbert was priested in 1630. Such was life. And poetry? This was, for a man of Herbert's formation and talents, a crisis about words – words used to show off and deceive, words used to tell the truth.

Herbert was in love with words. Just think of 'The Odour'. When we are children, words strike us like that: as inherently onomatopoeic, their very sounds sensuous spells and enchantments. Here, Herbert inhales the meaning out of words. In the first two stanzas he is alone in his voluptuous sniffing, then the meaning of 'my Master', and not just its sound, takes over and the mutuality of relationship and exchange is affirmed: 'And so this new commerce and sweet/ Should all my life [notice!] employ and busy me'.

I will conclude with 'The Forerunners'. The master metaphor is the chalking of doors for billeting by harbingers of an army or royal progress. Herbert's love of words is at its most sensuous in lines 19 and 20. Words are delicious. But what do they mean and do? That is a matter of communication with another and others, and should be plain and direct. We are indebted to Buck, the Cambridge printer of the first edition of *The Temple* for italicising that key phrase with its blunt monosyllables which is not, is even anti-, euphonious: '*Thou art still my God*'.

Helen Wilcox
Friday, 11th July
Sarum College

Herbert and the Material World

Prof Helen Wilcox is Head of the School of English at Bangor University (Wales). Her research interests lie mainly in Renaissance literature and she has published widely on seventeenth-century devotional poetry, women's writing, drama, autobiography, and the relationship of words and music. She is editor of the acclaimed annotated edition of *The English Poems of George Herbert* (Cambridge University Press, 2007) and co-editor of the essay collection *Locating George Herbert: Family; Place; Traditions*.

Herbert is frequently described as a metaphysical poet, but Helen argues that on closer study, his devotional poems are in fact firmly grounded in the physical environment, the material world. By reference to eight poems, Helen investigated the ways in which Herbert's verse works with earthly matter in order to explore spiritual experience, transforming (as Herbert himself put it) 'things of ordinary use' into 'lights even of heavenly truth'.

The poems Helen chose were: 'Gratefulnesse', lines 1-4; 'Praise (III)', lines 1-6; 'The Church-floore', lines 1-12; 'The Agonie'; 'The Windows'; 'Mattens'; 'The Elixir' and 'Vertue'.

She demonstrated how, through his use of metaphor, Herbert draws the reader beyond the physical to the spiritual, 'The Church-floore' providing a particularly good example. Ordinary things, the small scale and the familiar such as trees, water, air, weather and flowers, serve to illuminate spiritual truth. Herbert's references to the senses of smell, taste, and even to music in the stretched sinews of the strings against wood, all suggest that for him, the experience of God has to be felt; that out of the physical world comes the spiritual.

Above
Helen Wilcox

Helen recollects: 'On Friday afternoon I gave a talk on Herbert and the Material World, held at Sarum College. The room was not easy to speak in – it's wide rather than deep – and the talk took place at the sleepy time of a hot afternoon… but I did my best to galvanise the audience with thoughts about Herbert's engagement with the physical as well as the spiritual world. I especially valued the chance to talk about poems such as 'The Church-floore', 'Mattens' and 'The Elixir', suggesting that Herbert's sense of our material surroundings invariably leads to a glimpse of heaven.'

Of the Festival as a whole, Helen commented: 'The programme was a great delight with its mixture of large and small events, formal and informal, literary, spiritual and artistic, in such a splendid variety of locations. The warm sunny weather properly reflected the prevailing mood indoors, and… friendships were made and renewed through GH during those special days.'

'I enjoyed the Festival so much. It seemed to me a huge success, with such a splendid array of talent, some of it very distinguished, and wonderful audiences, mostly full to capacity and very enthusiastic.'

'What a wonderful, wonderful Festival! … Helen Wilcox's vigorous, engaging talks… what a glorious whirlwind!'

'[The Festival] was a most enjoyable event of very high quality… To have so fine an experience, plus Helen Wilcox's talks plus the concert in Wilton House felt to be a very special treat.'

'A Blaze of Crying Birds'

Colleen Wethered

Friday, 11th July

Sarum College

Colleen Wethered read English at St Anne's College, Oxford. She has an MA in Theology from Sarum College and is now a doctoral student at Bangor University supervised by Prof Helen Wilcox and Prof Tony Brown.

Opening her talk, Colleen suggested that there are common features in the work of Welsh poets George Herbert, R.S. Thomas and Rowan Williams. All dislike self-absorbed projections of God, all use metaphor to express spirituality and for all the writers, nature is a paradigm of the way God works.

Colleen chose Herbert's 'Easter-wings', Thomas's 'A Thicket in Lleyn' and Williams's 'September Birds' to examine how the use of bird metaphors reveals the song of the poet. Colleen took the title of her talk from 'Deathship' by Rowan Williams. Written on the death of R.S. Thomas, it represents a cross-over point between the three poets and their work.

In comparing 'A Thicket in Lleyn' with 'Easter-wings', Colleen observed that both poems are about recognition of the poet's role – to encourage us to look around us and see the imminence of the divine. Thus we internalise what we see, then we can be transformed. God is the primary inspiration, the artist is second. In 'Easter-wings', Herbert has experienced recognition and has internalised it; the poem gives us the inner workings, the difficulties of getting there. Thomas, on the other hand, gives us a chronological account of the process.

Like 'Easter-wings', 'September Birds' is a poem of Resurrection. It is set in a hidden place, as is 'A Thicket in Lleyn'. Yet here, the role of the poet is different. The sun – or the son of God – is the protagonist: the sun has affected the visual picture but the problem is our interpretation of that picture.

Above
Colleen Wethered

Herbert gives us the whole picture and says 'Let the poem reveal what it may'. Thomas has charted his way into a new way of feeling. Williams writes about the nature of revelation itself and the yielding of meaning, telling us that meaning is beyond articulation.

Colleen concluded by asking why Williams chooses to use the word 'blaze' about Thomas. She put forward several thoughts: the burning bush is a central image for Williams; Gillian Clarke in her poem dedicated to Thomas on his death refers to 'the one frail coracle, borne out to sea, burning'; Thomas explodes at times with humour; and finally 'blaze', for Colleen, has Welsh connotations, as embodied in sparks from flint and the Welsh landscape.

'A heartfelt thank you for the George Herbert Festival. It was a very special event, a veritable feast, your ambitious trawl of lecturers and speakers really delivered.'

'The three lectures I attended on the Friday and the walk to Bemerton on the Saturday were so worthwhile. I am a comparative newcomer to George Herbert and felt very blessed and privileged to be further familiarised with him.'

'I learnt so much from the talks and found the whole experience a great intellectual and spiritual stimulus.'

'Hearken unto a Verser'

**Gillian Clarke,
Andrew Motion
& Rowan Williams
with
Maggie Guillebaud,
Moderator**

Friday, 11th July

Salisbury Playhouse

'Thank you for this lovely event. It was a treat to hear Rowan Williams and Andrew Motion, especially, talk about poetry.'

Gillian Clarke was appointed National Poet for Wales in 2008. She is President of Ty Newydd, the Welsh Writers Centre which she co-founded in 1990. She has published ten collections of poems and a book of prose, *At the Source*. Her latest poetry collection, *Ice*, was shortlisted for the T.S. Eliot award, 2012. In 2010 she was awarded the Queen's Gold Medal for Poetry.

Sir Andrew Motion read English at University College, Oxford and subsequently spent two years writing about the poetry of Edward Thomas for his MLitt. After teaching English at the University of Hull, he edited The *Poetry Review* and then became Editorial Director and Poetry Editor at Chatto & Windus. He is now Professor of Creative Writing at Royal Holloway, University of London and is a Fellow of the Royal Society of Literature. He was Poet Laureate from 1999–2009 and was knighted for his services to literature in 2009.

Dr Rowan Williams's biography appears on page 10.

Maggie Guillebaud is an Anglican priest. Before becoming ordained, she had a varied career in public service including chairing an NHS trust, being a member of the Arts Council of England, chairing the Arts Council's regional arm for the South West and being a JP. She is a board member of the Ageas Salisbury International Arts Festival.

As a prologue to this poets' symposium, the final poetry event of the Festival, Tom Graves of Bishop Wordsworth's School (BWS) read the first verse of 'The Church-porch'. The poem, which includes the words 'Hearken unto a Verser', bids youth to find goodness in poetry.

Above - *The three poets (left to right)*
Gillian Clarke, Andrew Motion and Rowan Williams
Picture courtesy of Salisbury Journal

Above
Edward Piggott reading Herbert's
poem 'The Collar'.

Why does Herbert appeal to you?

Maggie asked each participant to give a brief, personal view on Herbert's poetry.

Gillian cited two qualities – the music of his poetry and the insight conferred by the reality of his imagery. For Andrew, Herbert's appeal lies in his use of simple language and a familiar world of reference, which he wraps around spiritual and rarified ideas. There is an immaculacy of form in the poems, a neatness, in contrast to what surrounds them. Rowan highlighted the tension Herbert creates between this 'neatness', and the outrageous and the subversive – for example through his use of chaos and uncertainty; and how the plain-room image forces you to face yourself.

The session continued by examining three poems: 'Vertue', 'The Collar' and 'Prayer (I)'.

'The trialogue on Friday evening with Rowan, Andrew Motion and Gillian Clarke [was] a wonderful balance of subtle literary criticism, sensitive theology and emotional intelligence, all within a gentle conversation among friends...'

**Gillian Clarke,
Andrew Motion
& Rowan Williams
with
Maggie Guillebaud,
Moderator**

Friday, 11th July

Salisbury Playhouse

'Vertue' (read by Tom Graves, BWS)

For Gillian, the poem shows that Herbert had mastered more than one language: Latin gives the beat of the line and Anglo-Saxon gives the monosyllables and the plainer, more honest vocabulary in a poem that contains few multi-syllable or abstract words. Rowan remarked on the song form (in Welsh, one word means both 'song' and 'poem') and that while the first three stanzas concern material things, it is the fourth, which does not, that is the toughest. For Andrew, the intellectual movement of the poem seems natural, so like ordinary talk that you can miss its profound content. Herbert's musicality allows subtle variations in the way the poem moves within its sound world.

'The Collar' (read by Edward Piggott, BWS)

Andrew declared this poem to be wonderful. The dialogue is powerfully described, and the wit well employed. He identified three stages in the verse: first, anger at being restrained; second, being brought to heel by a voice from elsewhere; and third, the surprise ending telling us that through child-likeness the moral compass is recovered. He sees the end not as a reversal; rather, the storm has blown out.

'The most memorable experience of the Festival for me was the full and varied contribution made by the former Archbishop of Canterbury, Dr Rowan Williams… he took part in the poets' discussion forum at the Playhouse – without notes, obviously knowing the poems by heart – and his contributions were unfailingly perceptive.'

'I loved the conversations between the three poet-thinkers on the Friday night. [The Festival] was a fantastic opportunity for stimulating discussions, and for meeting old and new friends. I was struck by the diverse people who had been touched by the work of George Herbert, and the spirit with which they came together to discuss it.'

'Prayer (I)' (read by Tom Graves)

Prayer, Maggie affirmed, was central to Herbert's life, and he regarded prayer and preaching as having equal importance.

Rowan highlighted the breadth and passion of Herbert's imagery: 'Gods breath in man'; 'Christ-side-piercing spear'; 'Church-bels' summoning God from 'beyond the starres'. Yet the ending – 'something understood' – he suggested has a Shakespearian quality of prosaic simplicity; you get the point, you are enlightened. For Gillian, the litany of metaphors leading to 'something understood' represents the perfect definition of poetry. For Andrew, 'something understood' could be read either as something good, something that has been resolved, or, less satisfyingly, as 'only something, not everything'. He argued that the poem is testament to Herbert's realism, the power of the verse lying in the oscillation between things far off and those near at hand. Rounding off the discussion, Rowan posited a further interpretation of the words 'Heaven in ordinarie' – an 'ordinarie' being a seventeenth-century pub!

'Some of the details that I appreciated were the lovely introductions to each of the sessions… [and] the carefully thought-out questions posed to the panel on Friday evening…'

Above
The poets on stage with Maggie Guillebaud

25

Who was George Herbert?

Sonia Woolley

Saturday, 12th July

Sarum College

Sonia Woolley is a professional actress and director. For many years she was a regular member of the Salisbury Playhouse company, she has appeared in the West End and she has directed Benjamin Britten operas at Salisbury Cathedral, one of which was televised by the BBC. Now also working as a freelance consultant in voice and presentation skills, she is a member of the Voice Care Network (UK) and runs workshops for groups as varied as teachers, churches and businesses. She has been a frequent contributor to the Summer Evenings with George Herbert series in Salisbury.

Illustrated by readings of his prose, poetry and the works of his biographers, Sonia's talk took her audience on a brief journey through the life of Herbert, who spent the final and creatively important three years of his life in Salisbury as Rector of Fugglestone-cum-Bemerton.

Commenting on the experience, Sonia observed: 'It was a great privilege to have been involved in a festival with such illustrious participants and eager audiences. The response to my session seemed extremely positive. It included a compilation of details about Herbert's personal background, the different structures used in his poetry and extracts from 'The Church-porch'. Walton's biography gave an added prose dimension. The description and examples of Herbert's influence on Vikram Seth's writing also seemed of particular interest to the audience.'

'Thank you again for a few days which have given my mind and spirit a meditative gentleness which I will draw on for a long while.'

As well as giving her own talk, Sonia read some of Herbert's verse at Dr Rowan Williams's session, 'Why Herbert Matters' and at the 'One Harmonie' concert in the Double Cube Room at Wilton House.

'For me,' said Sonia of Festival as a whole, 'the personal highlights were lively conversations with Bishop Nicholas and Archbishop Rowan in the Playhouse Green Room before the Thursday event, and the unique experience of performing in the Double Cube Room with such wonderful music and atmosphere!'

Above
Sonia Woolley
presenting her talk
in the Cavell Room,
Sarum College

Left
The nineteenth-century engraving of George Herbert in his Old Rectory bedroom, illustrating the poem 'Employment (I)'

'How does one thank you for bringing about such a wonderful experience as the George Herbert Festival? I am sure you will never know how significant the event has been in the lives of many people, mine included. Thank you!'

'The Festival was an inspiration to us. Not only did we discover so much more about George Herbert's poetry writing, and the wonders of different places around Salisbury, but our minds were stretched, our spirits lifted and, at our advancing years, a fresh hope given to our lives. And what a coup to have the performance in the Cube Room at Wilton. The associations there with George Herbert are so appropriate. Thank you for all that.'

27

Helen Wilcox

Saturday, 12th July

Wilton House

Herbert, the Sidneys and the Psalms

Prof Helen Wilcox's biography is on page 18.

The Sidney Psalms formed the single most important poetic influence on Herbert's devotional verse. The translation of the Psalms into English verse was begun by Philip Sidney before his death in 1586, and completed in 1595 by his sister, Mary Sidney Herbert, wife of the second Earl of Pembroke. Courtesy of the Earl and Countess of Pembroke and the Trustees, the talk took place in the Wilton House's Double Cube Room.

Helen explored Herbert's poetry in the light of its relationship with the Bible and the Sidney Psalms, bringing alive these vibrant poetic partnerships in Wilton House, the home of Mary Sidney and, in the subsequent generation, Herbert's patrons.

'On Saturday afternoon,' Helen recalls, 'I was privileged to give the final talk of the Festival in the sumptuous surroundings of the Double Cube Room, under the gaze of countless magnificent van Dyck paintings on the walls around me and numerous cherubs on the ceiling above.

'Herbert scholar Helen Wilcox gave two very fine lectures, one on Herbert's poems and the Psalms written by Mary and Philip Sidney.'

Above
Helen Wilcox speaking in front of the van Dyck painting of Herbert's kinsman, the fourth Earl of Pembroke and his family

28

'I took this opportunity to argue that the most important influence on Herbert as poet was not only the Biblical Psalms but also the verse translation of the Psalms by the talented Elizabethan brother and sister, Philip and Mary Sidney. The translation was completed by Mary Sidney while she was living at Wilton, married to the second Earl of Pembroke; it was a great delight to me that her present-day successor, the current Countess of Pembroke, was sitting in the front row as I spoke. This was a lovely link, especially as I was also claiming Mary Sidney's importance as a crucial example for subsequent English women poets as well as for Herbert.

'The rhetorical and metrical skills to be observed in the Sidney translation of the Psalms are very close to the stanzaic variety and exquisite tones of Herbert's *Temple*, and I was pleased to be able to demonstrate this with examples from both collections. From the seventeenth century onwards, Herbert was often referred to as the "sweet singer of the temple" who followed in David's footsteps, and during the talk I explored some of the Psalm-like qualities of his poems.

'Typically, Herbert was also well aware of the impossible challenge of writing a "true" hymn or Psalm and agonised about the process even as he succeeded so well in it! Mary Sidney's work was clearly a very positive example for him as he set about constructing his own "book of stars" to light the way to heaven.'

'I write to thank and congratulate all those who organised the wonderful George Herbert Festival… It was a most enjoyable event of high quality… To have so fine an experience including Helen Wilcox's talks and the concert in Wilton felt to be a very special treat.'

'Having poems read before they were discussed and having so many poems printed in advance (e.g. at Helen Wilcox's talks) were other marks of professionalism…'

Above
Judy Rees welcoming the Countess of Pembroke and Trustees of Wilton House to Helen Wilcox's talk

Poetry Discussion Groups

Leaders:
Dr Beth Dodd,
Dr John Drury,
Rev Canon David Durston,
Prof Chris Hodgkins,
Prof Greg Miller,
Sir Andrew Motion,
Rev Canon Mark Oakley,
Prof Helen Wilcox &
Dr Rowan Williams

Friday, 11th &
Saturday, 12th July

Prof Chris Hodgkins is Professor of Renaissance Literature at the University of North Carolina – Greensboro. Author and editor of four books on George Herbert and on seventeenth-century literature, he is also co-founder of the George Herbert Society, which organises events in Britain, Europe and North America. With Robert Whalen, he co-edits *The Digital Temple* and has started work on *The Complete Digital Works of George Herbert*. He directs UNCG's Atlantic World Research Network; he has published extensively on the British imperial imagination, and is completing a book on the literary study of the Bible.

Prof Greg Miller is the Janice C. Trimble Professor of English at Millsaps College, Jackson, Mississippi. He is the author of a number of books including *George Herbert's 'Holy Patterns': Reforming Individuals in Community* (Continuum, 2007). He has also written for the *George Herbert Journal* and has published a collection of his own poetry, *The Sea Sleeps: New and Selected Poems* (Paraclete Press, 2014).

Biographies for Dr Beth Dodd, Dr John Drury, Sir Andrew Motion, Rev Canon Mark Oakley, Prof Helen Wilcox and Dr Rowan Williams appear on pages 14, 16, 22, 57, 18 and 10 respectively.

'…my discussion group with Mark Oakley was very thought provoking. The hospitality at 31 The Close for the discussion group was very pleasant and enhancing of the event. Thank you for all your efforts on behalf of this.'

Over two days, ten poetry discussion groups took place in homes and other venues around Salisbury, each focusing on a different poem. Welcoming everyone, whatever their previous experience of Herbert, the groups aimed to develop a deeper mutual understanding and appreciation of Herbert's works. The groups studied 'The Collar' (with David Durston), 'Deniall' (with Helen Wilcox), 'Easter-wings' (with Beth Dodd), 'The Flower' (with Mark Oakley), 'The Pearl' (with Chris Hodgkins), 'The Altar' (with Andrew Motion), 'Affliction (I)' (with John Drury), 'The Pulley' (with Mark Oakley) and 'Love (III)' (with Rowan Williams).

Each attracting between seven and fifteen people, the 90-minute sessions proved memorable for many – both participants and leaders.

Helen Wilcox recollects 'As a contributor, I was involved in three events. The first was one of the poetry groups, which as a series formed the backbone of the Festival. They went on quietly and unobtrusively each day, and everyone who attended had the chance to participate informally and equally. My group met on Friday morning at Eleanor Wordsworth's elegant home. There were 15 of us, ranging from teenagers to senior citizens – including students, musicians, clergy, artists, lecturers and a psychologist – and it was clear that almost everyone in the group had chosen to read Herbert's poems for pleasure. All were evidently engaged by the poem we had been assigned – 'Deniall' – and everyone spoke at some point during the wide-ranging discussion. There was lively exchange of views on poetry, prayer, the human body and the experience of exclusion, and in the end we particularly focused on the paradoxes of Herbert's art in its combination of order and dynamic energy. We were busy for nearly two hours and even then didn't share everything we could have said about the poem, nor did we have time to read out the poem again at the end as we had hoped. Still, discussion is an ongoing thing and it was very appropriate to leave Ellie's house still feeling as though we would see yet more in the poem on our next reading of it ...'

'I was lucky enough to be part of the discussion group led by Sir Andrew Motion and it has increased my appreciation of George Herbert's poetry, introduced me to the work of other poets influenced by him and prompted me to explore other avenues. Everyone I spoke to had high praise for every event they had attended – thank you!'

Above
One of the small poetry discussion groups in session, led by Prof Chris Hodgkins (third from left)

Festival Garden Party

Above: *Group photo of Garden Party hosts and guests*

Middle: *Hostess Helen Holtam (left) with a group of guests*

Below: *Host Bishop Nicholas Holtam with Judy Rees*

Right:
A group
of Garden
Party guests

Left: *Salisbury Cathedral Precentor Tom Clammer and Rowan Williams*

Musical Spaces in *The Temple*

Simon Jackson with Marcus Tomalin, Lute

Friday, 11th July

Sarum College

Dr Simon Jackson is Organist and Director of Music at Little St Mary's, Cambridge. In 2011 he completed his doctoral research on The Literary and Musical Activities of the Herbert Family.

Herbert's *The Temple* is celebrated as much for its architectural properties as its musical verse. Simon examined how these two strands of poetic technique combine. Accompanied by lutenist Dr Marcus Tomalin, he took his audience on a tour of the musical and acoustic spaces that are encountered in Herbert's life and verse, punctuated by the music that Herbert found in each place.

Sound and space are important aspects of Herbert's work, shaping his poems and his hymns. Simon demonstrated that *The Temple* takes the reader through the church building, integrating the visual and the aural, the spatial and the musical. The concept of 'harmony', he argued, offers one way to achieve this as it allows a bridge to be built between music and poetry – the harmony of a space expressing a rationality, a fingerprint of God's creation.

'To hear contemporary lute music, and have some experts talk on it, were unexpected treats.'

Harmony in pattern and form

Simon pointed out that Herbert arranges his words in mathematical proportions, and music and poetry meet in this frame. Herbert's pattern poems, for instance, which are pleasing to the eye and to the ear, provide a synthetic understanding of the world that reflects its divine ordering. Harmony was, of course, also reflected in contemporaneous architecture and garden design – the garden at Wilton House, for example, was a study in proportion – and the fountains and water provided music to the poetic ear.

Above
*Simon Jackson with
lutenist Marcus Tomalin*

Herbert's use of sound and space

Herbert took inspiration for the music of his poetry from real places, events and ambient sounds – for example the mapped landscape, country pastimes such as the Rogation procession and the chatter of birds.

He also knew how to match sound to space. In this, he reveals an understanding of acoustics, as in the call and response elements of Antiphon (I) where music, space and text interact. The changes he made to his church at Leighton Bromswold in the 1620s – replacing the dirt floor with tiles, and installing a pulpit and reading desk with sounding boards – underline his awareness of practical acoustics.

Small, private spaces also feature in *The Temple* – boxes, walled gardens, cells etc, leading to thoughts of private devotion. Simon suggested that Herbert himself may have spent time in such places meditating on the lute, giving rise to metaphors such as 'fretting in the Psalms'. Herbert was, in Simon's view, most likely to have played psalmody in the Genevan tradition, and features of Herbert's poetry, for instance feminine endings, could derive from his writing words to existing music of this genre.

During the talk, Marcus Tomalin played two pieces from the 1620 Lute Book of Lord Edward Herbert of Cherbury, brother of George.

Concluding, Simon argued that the concept of shared space that is embodied in Herbert's poetry is consistent with the communality, the 'shared ground', of Christianity as a whole.

Above
Marcus Tomalin tunes his lute before the event

'Simon Jackson's talk was tremendous; the level of quality was so high. I would love to read his script!'

'God Almighty Planted a Garden'

Presented by Words and Music, with Sally Bradshaw, Soprano; Michael Haslam, Piano; & Rowan Williams, Reader

Friday, 11th July

St John's Church, Bemerton

Words and Music is a flexible, vocally based ensemble which devises a wide range of programmes on specific themes. They have appeared for the National Portrait Gallery in a show devised for the Byron exhibition, for the British Council on tour to the Far East and in Europe, for the Cambridge Festival in *Cambridge Eccentrics*, and nationwide in *1000 Years of Christmas* for theatres including the Stephen Joseph, Scarborough, the Theatre Royal, Bath and many others.

Sally Bradshaw has sung in concerts, opera and recordings throughout the world. She has recorded Handel roles, notably Agrippina for Harmonia Mundi, as well as Debussy songs for Warner and many contemporary pieces. Judith Weir, Alec Roth, Howard Skempton and Nicola Lefanu have all written music for her, much of which has been recorded. She teaches singing at Cambridge University and in France.

Michael Haslam is known as a virtuosic pianist as well as an accomplished music director. He has directed musical shows at the National Theatre and the Royal Opera House. He is also known for arrangements and was the musical director and arranger of Maria Friedman's one-woman show and of Miriam Margolyes' 'Dickens' Women'.

Dr Rowan Williams's biography appears on page 10.

Above
*Rowan Williams delivering
one of the readings*

*Picture courtesy of
James Woods*

'Sally's singing was exquisite. What a pleasure to hear her voice counter posed with the poetry! And Michael Haslam's accompaniment was so sensitive. Altogether a joy to listen to!'

This lunchtime recital set out to illustrate how the plant kingdom was reflected in the writings and musical compositions of George Herbert and his contemporaries. This was a period when formal gardens were increasing in popularity, and Herbert's stepfather Sir John Danvers had laid out a particularly fine example of the Italian-style of garden at his house in Chelsea. Francis Bacon, who did much to arouse popular interest in the natural sciences, was a friend of the Herbert family and undoubtedly would have had an influence on Herbert's understanding of the physical world, as created by God.

So Francis Bacon provided a perfect introduction to the event (and its title). A reading from his essay 'Of Gardens' was followed by extracts from the works of Andrew Marvell and John Milton, and Herbert's poem 'Paradise'. These readings were interspersed with contemporary music by Peter Warlock and Henry Lawes.

The next few pieces changed the subject to trees, starting with a reading from Shakespeare's *Hamlet* about the willow, followed by readings from Herbert and Thomas Newton, and songs by Grainger and Coleman. Herbert was interested in horticulture and was well aware of how to prune the fruit trees in the grounds of the Old Rectory to promote healthy growth, a process he exemplifies in 'Paradise'.

He was also familiar with the medicinal properties of herbs and plants, so the next reading of 'The Parson as Healer' from his book *The Country Parson* was especially appropriate. The ability to make potions and salves, and employ natural remedies, was essential knowledge for someone in

his position in a rural community without physicians. Other readings in this section were taken from the works of Ben Jonson, with musical settings by William Lawes and Roger Quilter.

Flowers came next, with modern composer Alec Roth's interpretation of Herbert's 'The Flower', the setting of Robert Herrick's well-known verse 'To the Virgins, To Make Much of Time' ('Gather ye rosebuds, while ye may') by William Lawes, and Benjamin Britten's composition 'For the flowers are great blessings' from 'Rejoice in the Lamb', a setting of Christopher Smart's 'Jubilate Agno'.

A reading of several stanzas from George Herbert's 'Providence', his major poem about the natural world, and Ralph Vaughan Williams's setting of his poem 'Easter' ('I got me flowers') provided a fitting conclusion to a well-constructed programme, expertly performed by Sally Bradshaw, Michael Haslam and Rowan Williams.

Above

Sally Bradshaw singing during the lunchtime concert, accompanied by Michael Haslam

Picture courtesy of James Woods

'Dancing Proverbs'

**Barry Ferguson
& Paris Helen**

Saturday, 12th July

Sarum College

Barry Ferguson was advised by his mentor, the composer Herbert Howells, to 'Meet interesting people!'. He has been blessed by meeting many such people: Reginald Moore, his Director of Music at Exeter Cathedral; Stanley Vann, the choir trainer at Peterborough Cathedral to whom he was assistant in the 1960s; friendships with numerous others including music colleagues at Rochester Cathedral where he was Organist and Master of the Choristers from 1977–94; George Herbert and Thomas Hardy devotees; plus a lifelong succession of muses, none more so than his artist wife Sandi and professional violinist daughter Rachel.

Paris Helen began teaching dance in North Dorset in 1992. Her professional theatre career started when she was 14 and still at school, singing in the chorus of a summer season at Glyndebourne. She celebrated her 18th birthday whilst dancing with Sadlers Wells Opera Company in a Handel festival. Paris is currently a freelance dance teacher and choreographer, and she organises the International Summer School for Young Dancers.

'The music [in the Festival] was especially important to us. TWO new compositions – well, three if you count Barry's revised settings for the dance… Thank you for all that.'

Right
Paris Helen interpreting Barry Ferguson's music inspired by Herbert's collection of proverbs

Barry Ferguson had long admired Herbert's *Outlandish Proverbs*. Having been inspired by watching Paris Helen take a ballet class and demonstrate movements, he realised that the *Proverbs* provided an ideal starting point for the ten piano pieces he then wrote for her. Paris responded with flair and imagination. David Hilliam, writer and lecturer, wrote a scholarly script to accompany the work, but sadly he died shortly before the first performance in 2012. This second performance, with a revised script, was dedicated to David's memory.

A full house was treated to a memorable blend of music and movement. As one audience member put it, 'I particularly enjoyed the combination of music and dance in "Dancing Proverbs", when Barry Ferguson's piano pieces… were interpreted in movement by the elegant dancer Paris Helen. The idea of "dancing without movement" contained in one of the proverbs was movingly associated with the experience of the deaf who respond in dance to the vibrations set up by music. This movement was requested as an encore and gave rise to profound thoughts about music, silence and hopefulness.'

'I enjoyed the tension and audacity of the whole idea' observed another. 'Proverbs are pragmatic, grown from the daily experience of being human. Music lifts us into another dimension. Yet it reveals the poetry of life in unexpected places – "he that goeth far hath many encounters"… I particularly like "he that liveth in hope danceth without music" where the accompaniment is trying so delicately not to be there. And the boisterous ones about storms and soldiers. Even in a small space you can make a to-do! Thank you so much.'

Before the tenth and final proverb was danced, Barry concluded 'Thank God for George Herbert – and this Festival. Thank God for love, which like the Arts, shines like a candle in the world.'

'Love makes one fitt for any work.'
(Outlandish Proverbs)

Above
Composer Barry Ferguson introducing the event in the Sarum College Chapel

'One Harmonie'

The Farrant Singers, Conductor – Andrew Mackay; Alison Hill, Soprano; Reiko Ichise, Viol; Elizabeth Kenny, Lute; and Nigel Wingate & Sonia Woolley, Readers

Saturday, 12th July

Wilton House

'The music, especially the renderings of Blow and Purcell by the young soloist and the new pieces by Barry Ferguson and Alec, formed a fitting climax to an extremely successful Festival.'

The Farrant Singers was founded in 1958 by the composer Richard Lloyd, then Assistant Organist at Salisbury Cathedral. Andrew Mackay took up the baton in 2011. With around 38 singers, its repertoire includes a wide range of sacred and secular music spanning may periods and styles. The Farrants featured on BBC Radio 4's 'Sunday Worship' in a service dedicated to George Herbert broadcast live from St Andrew's, Bemerton.

Alison Hill began singing as a chorister at Salisbury Cathedral, graduating from Trinity College, Cambridge in 2006. She continues to study with Ashley Stafford and Philip Doghan. Since 2009 she has recorded and toured extensively with ensembles including The Monteverdi Choir under Sir John Eliot Gardiner, Polyphony under Stephen Layton and The Sixteen for Harry Christophers.

Reiko Ichise was born in Tokyo and read musicology at Kunitachi College of Music where she started playing viols. She came to the UK to pursue her studies with Richard Boothby. Now established as one of the leading viol players in the UK, she regularly performs with many prominent early music ensembles and orchestras. Reiko is a professor at the Royal College of Music.

Elizabeth Kenny is one of Europe's leading lute players. She is a principal with the Orchestra of the Age of Enlightenment, and her research interests have led her to critically acclaimed recordings of Lawes, Purcell and Dowland, and to the formation of her ensemble Theatre of the Ayre. She is an artistic advisor to the York Early Music Festival, Professor of Lute at the Royal College of Music and a Reader in Performance at Southampton University.

Above - *The Farrant singers under their conductor Andrew Mackay taking applause at the end of the concert*

Above
Alison Hill

Herbert's life, work and legacy were brought together in this atmospheric concert, the final event of the Festival. With the kind permission of the Earl and Countess of Pembroke and the Trustees, the Double Cube Room at Wilton House provided a venue that was both splendid and fitting.

Beneath van Dyck's portrait of Herbert's antecedents, a capacity audience was treated to settings of Herbert's words composed across almost four centuries. Interposed with the music was a selection of his poetry, read by Sonia Woolley and Nigel Wingate, together with extracts from writings about Herbert, all of which combined to illustrate Herbert's enduring impact on composers and writers over this period.

The evening was exceptionally hot and still. Yet the audience remained rapt throughout the exquisitely performed and well-chosen programme.

'There was a moment during the concert when I looked out of the window while Ali was singing to the soft strains of the lute', commented a Farrant singer. 'Suddenly it felt as if I was at a seventeenth-century gathering and would not have been surprised to turn back and find everyone in period dress, listening as intently to the music of their day as we were all listening centuries later.'

The Farrant Singers, Conductor
– Andrew Mackay;
Alison Hill, Soprano;
Reiko Ichise, Viol;
Elizabeth Kenny, Lute;
and Nigel Wingate & Sonia Woolley, Readers

Saturday, 12th July

Wilton House

Above
Reiko Ichise

Elizabeth Kenny later recalled, 'It was very moving to play in this evocative place. And "Awake my lute and struggle for thy part" reminded me that Herbert had first-hand experience of trying to stay in tune and play the right notes!'

In reviewing the concert, Stuart Robinson said in the *Salisbury Journal* (17.7.14), 'There was some excellent playing and singing from the Farrant Singers…, soprano soloist Alison Hill and Elizabeth Kenny (lute). Each piece was helpfully preceded by the reading of the text.'

Two works received their premieres on this occasion, Barry Ferguson's setting of 'Prayer (I)' and Alec Roth's 'Men and Angels'. Of these, the *Journal* said:

'Alec Roth's "Men and Angels" [is] a clever setting of the dialogue between angels and man in praise of God. Roth's writing is lush with melodic close harmonies. "Prayer (I)" by Shaftesbury-based composer Barry Ferguson is an imaginative setting of Herbert's insight into the fragmentary nature of prayer. Ferguson's sonorities are more sparse but lyrical nonetheless. The Farrant Singers did credit to them both.'

Capturing the mood of the performers, a Farrant member (and architect) later reflected 'As I was singing and listening, as with many performances in great buildings, I thought of the nearly 400-year-old history of the room (designed by Inigo Jones and John Webb in 1653) and how many people had over the centuries performed, listened and enjoyed their own brand of culture and entertainment in that famous space. And here we were, in 2014, adding to that history with a celebration of the work of a local and equally famous intellectual. Andy directed and brought the choir to a standard we have rarely reached. It was a privilege to take part.'

'The Festival was a great success,' observed Alec Roth later, 'and I was delighted that I was able to contribute in some way. I thought the Wilton concert was a wonderful way to round things off.'

'What really made the evening for me was hearing
Herbert's words so beautifully spoken and having
the tremendous privilege of singing two new settings
in the presence of the composers.'

Left - *Composers Alec Roth
(left) and Barry Ferguson
(right) following the first
public performance of their
new settings of Herbert's
verse*

Above
Elizabeth Kenny

Above: *Festival goers enjoy the picnic on the Bemerton recreation ground beside the River Nadder*

Middle: *An official guide briefing the Saturday afternoon audience prior to their tour of Wilton House*

Below: *A visitor reading Herbert's verse during the drop-in at St Andrew's Church, Bemerton*

Right: *Poetry reading during the drop-in at St Peter's Church, Fugglestone*

Left: *Helen Wilcox addressing her audience in the Double Cube Room at Wilton House*

'Espying Heav'n'

Adrian Barlow

Saturday, 12th July

Sarum College

Above
*Detail of the Herbert window
by Charles Eamer Kempe in the
church at Bishop Burton, Yorkshire
Picture courtesy of Adrian Barlow*

Adrian Barlow retired in 2011 as Director of Public and Professional Programmes at the University of Cambridge Institute of Continuing Education. He is particularly interested in Victorian architecture and ecclesiology, and is writing a book on the stained glass of Charles Eamer Kempe. He is President of the English Association, and George Herbert and his poetry have always meant a great deal to him.

'In my talk,' Adrian recalled 'I wanted to focus on three things. First, I discussed some of the contrasting post-Reformation attitudes to stained glass that Herbert would have encountered, especially at Cambridge; in doing so, I explained how his own college chapel at Trinity (only 45 years old when he went up as an undergraduate) had no stained glass at all, while King's College Chapel had the finest and largest set of modern stained glass in England, if not in Europe. I speculated that looking at the glass in King's – especially at the small internal windows in the Chapel – would have enabled Herbert to observe the techniques by which glaziers created the wonderful effects of radiant colour that are the hallmarks of stained glass.

'Second, I suggested that it was by looking closely at such glass that Herbert began to see its value as symbol and metaphor, and to integrate words such as "anneal", "brittle", "waterish" and "light" itself into his poetic vocabulary. This gave me the opportunity to introduce into my lecture discussion of poems, not only those as well-known as 'The Elixir', but also 'Mattens' and 'The Windows'.

'I learned a lot from this excellent lecture, especially about the stages of Herbert's reputation as indicated by the figures with whom he was paired in the window designs, from Laud to Bunyan!'

'The third objective of my lecture was to discuss the ways in which Herbert himself, in the nineteenth and twentieth centuries, was represented (or "annealed" to use one of his own favourite glass-making terms) by different artists in stained glass windows. I explored the extent to which every image depends upon the posthumous portrait of Herbert by Robert White (1674) and draws upon the description of the poet by Izaac Walton: "He was for his person of a stature inclining towards tallness; his body was very straight, and so far from being cumbered with too much flesh, that he was lean to an extremity. His aspect was cheerful…"

'I was pleased to be able to introduce the audience to at least two stained glass images they had not seen before: the first (from the Cheltenham Ladies' College) depicted Herbert in his church at Bemerton, and the second (a "lost" portrait from the studio of Charles Eamer Kempe) which had originally been in Kempe's own home, Old Place in Sussex, but which I tracked down – to Church House in Salisbury itself! No one, in fact, produced more stained glass images of Herbert than Kempe, for whom I have great admiration. Indeed, it was an unexpected bonus of speaking in Sarum College that I was able to encourage my audience to go upstairs to see the fine Kempe E. window in the Chapel – a discovery for me too!'

Above
Detail of the Herbert Window in the chapel of Herbert's alma mater Trinity College, Cambridge depicting him with John Donne and Francis Bacon

Picture courtesy of Trinity College, Cambridge

Left
Adrian Barlow

'Studie this Art'

Sandi Ferguson
Friday, 11th and
Saturday, 12th July

Sarum College

Sandi Ferguson taught Art in England and abroad, and has designed sets and costumes for theatre and opera. Her passion for fabrics is reflected in quilting and she has exhibited in Dorset Art Weeks. For as long as she can remember, she has designed greetings cards and her card depicting George Herbert's 'The Flower' has been sent worldwide.

Sandi ran two 90-minute art workshops during which participants created their own cards depicting flowers and herbs that would have been familiar to George Herbert.

'It delighted me to lead the two workshops,' Sandi recollects. 'As usual, there was a mixture of abilities and some anxious faces at the start.

'After a brief introduction on flower drawing and painting, and the development into design, people selected a flower and materials. My local florist had arranged a magnificent collection of flowers and herbs that George Herbert would have known.

'The one-and-a-half hours flew by, but everyone left with a completed card. They were inspired by the beauty of the flowers and close observation of their form and colour, and were surprised by the standard they achieved in such a short time.'

'Sandi's encouraging enthusiasm was a real inspiration. I never thought I would come away with something I was so proud of!'

'The art workshop was such a treat. Using flowers of Herbert's time was a good idea. It made me feel more connected to his world.'

Above
Artist Sandi Ferguson showing an example of her work

from The Flower
by George Herbert

How fresh, O Lord, how sweet and clean
Are thy returns! ev'n as the flowers in spring;
To which, besides their own demean,
The late-past frosts tributes of pleasure bring.
            Grief melts away
            Like snow in May,
As if there were no such cold thing.

Who would have thought my shrivel'd heart
Could have recover'd greennesse? It was gone
    Quite under ground; as flowers depart
To see their mother-root, when they have blown;
            Where they together
            All the hard weather,
Dead to the world, keep house unknown.

And now in age I bud again,
After so many deaths I live and write;
I once more smell the dew and rain,
And relish versing: O my onely light,
            It cannot be
            That I am he
On whom thy tempests fell all night.

These are thy wonders, Lord of love,
To make us see we are but flowers that glide:
    Which when we once can finde and prove,
Thou hast a garden for us, where to bide.
            Who would be more,
            Swelling through store,
Forfeit their Paradise by their pride.

'[The speakers and session leaders] were outstanding – and delighted in imparting to each of us the joy of their discoveries about poetry, Herbert, art, and life.'

Above
Sandi Ferguson's card illustrating Herbert's poem 'The Flower'

'To Write a Verse'

Marion McKenzie

Friday, 11th and
Saturday, 12th July

Sarum College

Marion McKenzie studied calligraphy at Roehampton University. She teaches both privately and in adult education, takes commissions and has exhibited both locally and nationally. She is an elected Fellow of both the Society of Scribes and Illuminators, and the Calligraphy and Lettering Arts Society, of which she is currently Chairman.

Marion's workshops were offered on two days, giving around 20 people some practical insights into the art of calligraphy. The sessions began by looking at handwriting in Herbert's time. Marion then taught her students how to produce 'uncial' script, an uncomplicated yet pleasing characture that is well suited to poetry and is made up entirely of capital letters.

As no previous experience was needed to take part in the sessions, many participants thoroughly enjoyed the chance to indulge long-held wishes and have a go at this craft. Impressively, over two-and-a-half hours, they learned to write a whole uncial alphabet and at least one stanza of a Herbert poem of their choice.

'Thank you for a truly inspiring Festival. It really was a joy to have such a choice of top-quality and imaginative events.'

'I chose the calligraphy workshop on something of a whim but how glad I was! It was so very interesting and absorbing and Marion's knowledge and skill were very impressive.'

Above
Marion MacKenzie

50

'I have always had the idea that calligraphy would be fun, and Marion certainly whetted my appetite to do more!'

Left
*Marion MacKenzie
demonstrating the art of
the calligrapher to
Marcus Tomalin*

51

Left: *Prof Chris Hodgkins views the George Herbert display in the foyer of Salisbury Playhouse*

Right: *Pam Court (left), Festival Administrator, and Lesley Burton (right), Festival Secretary, staffing the information point at the Garden Party*

Right: *Festival Co-Chairman Peter Webster (left) and Wilton House Manager Nigel Bailey (right) prepare for the Saturday evening concert*

Below: *Sarum College Bookshop Manager Jenny Monds at the sales table in Salisbury Playhouse*

Above: Composer Barry Ferguson hard at work

53

Rowan Williams

Friday, 11th July

St Andrew's Church, Bemerton

Blessing of the George Herbert Stone

Dr Rowan Williams's biography appears on page 10.

To mark the Festival, a stone plaque commemorating George Herbert was most generously worked and donated by stonemason Robyn Golden-Hann. Bearing the words 'Love bade me welcome' – a quote from Herbert's well-known poem 'Love (III)' – the circular plaque now sits to the right of the doorway into St Andrew's Church, Bemerton, one of Herbert's two churches when he was Rector of Fuggelstone-cum-Bemerton from 1630–33.

On the morning of Friday, 11th July, the stone was blessed by Rowan Williams, who then presided at Communion in the church. 'It was a special service that morning,' recalls Simon Woodley, Rector of Bemerton. 'It was without pomp or complexity; no sermon nor hymn, just the same words we all say and always say – yet because of Rowan and the utter uniqueness of the occasion, and the intent of all present, it was an experience that will last with me for a long time.'

The stone used for the carving was a gift from Salisbury Cathedral. It is Chilmark stone, from which the Cathedral itself was built. 'The stone is about connections and gifts in many ways,' Simon explained. 'Firstly, it is a sign of welcome to any and all – we give this church as a place of rest or peace to people. Those seeking the George Herbert connection are reassured they have found the right place. It also binds two places special to George Herbert – the Cathedral and St Andrew's, through sharing the stone. Finally, it links the other church in the parish, St Michael's, as this is the place where the stonemason worships, and she has given the gift of time and talent for God's glory.'

Above

Detail of the plaque carved by stonemason Robyn Golden-Hann

Picture courtesy of Robyn Golden-Hann

Above - *Rowan Williams blessing the new carved stone in the porch of St Andrew's Church, Bemerton*
Picture courtesy of Salisbury Journal

'A large number of visitors from all over the world come to the church, and it is a delight to have these words of welcome, carved so beautifully, to greet them as they arrive.'

Services in Salisbury Cathedral

**Thursday, 10th
– Sunday 13th July**

Salisbury Cathedral

During the Festival, services held in the Cathedral referenced in different ways the life and work of George Herbert.

For Choral Evensong from Thursday to Sunday and for Choral Mattins on Sunday morning, David Halls, the Cathedral's Director of Music, selected music reflecting Herbert's ministry and influence, and that of his contemporaries. The schemes included, for instance, Vaughan Williams's 'The Call' and 'Antiphon'. David's own setting of Herbert's 'The Window', specially written for the Festival, was sung at the Evensong service on 10th July.

At the Festival Eucharist on Sunday, 13th July, the sermon was preached by the Rev Canon Mark Oakley, Chancellor of St Paul's Cathedral. Mark later recalled, 'The Eucharist was very well attended and included the hymns 'Teach me, my God and King' and 'King of Glory, King of Peace' as well as Vaughan Williams's haunting setting of 'Love (III)'. In the sermon I tried to show why both Herbert's understanding of God as his friend and the poet's remedies for the curses of literalism are both essential in the present day.'

Extracts of Mark's sermon are given here with his kind permission.

'…the man Salisbury has been celebrating over the last few days was a man very much tuned to heaven's humility. And his importance to a community of Christian faith in our present times, such as is gathered here now, is, I believe, vital.

'First, in a Googlesque world where knowledge is thought to be the same thing as information,… in a world restless for quick and easy headline answers, Herbert reminds us that if you are seeking God you need another language, in fact, a very different language. You need a language that is not ultimately about information but about formation, concerned as much with who you are turning into as with what you think you know; you need a language that exposes illusions but doesn't leave you disillusioned.

Above

*Festival Eucharist preacher
Rev Canon Mark Oakley,
Chancellor of St Paul's
Cathedral*

*Picture courtesy of
Graham Lacdoa*

Right
The quire of Salisbury Cathedral
Picture courtesy of Salisbury Cathedral
and Ash Mills

'You need a language that places space and silence around things, around words themselves, so that you learn through the disclosure and dislocation of silence to distrust the first impression that is so seasoned with your own prejudice, and enter a distillation process, where the familiar becomes strange and full of intrigue and invitation. Herbert reminds us again and again that if you are a person of faith, if you are taking the search for God and truth seriously, then poetry is your native language.

'And secondly, Herbert uses that language to speak of a God who challenges the crass characterisations that force themselves into our limp religious imaginations at the moment… With an audacious familiarity, a direct honesty and a spiritual perception for deep *resonance* instead of passing *relevance*, Herbert introduces us to a God who is friend. …And because God is his friend you feel in Herbert's faith that no matter how much he thrashes about and loses it like some restless adolescent, salvation is secure, forgiveness is unconditional, grace is irresistible. He's held and for always. The intimacy with God that we spy on in his poems comes from a confidence in the inviolability of their relationship. Again and again Herbert is speechless as he sees how much he is treasured.

'At the end of many of Herbert's poems the last few lines completely upturn all that you have been reading so far with fresh surprise. Just when you think your understanding of things is reaching a full stop he makes it a comma and more is shown and another chapter of love begins. [God takes the risk of stretching his arm out to us,] …as [he] did to Herbert, and only in that courageous desire to connect – in the face of all that could come between us – is a friendship and a future possible. Love took my hand. Smiling.'

George Herbert in the Schools

Both local junior and senior schools had a part in the Festival, with their own dedicated projects that involved children and young people from across Salisbury.

Junior school 'Flower' project

Pupils of Bemerton St John C of E Primary School took part in a competition based on Herbert's poem 'The Flower'. Children were encouraged to reflect on the beauty of nature that George Herbert describes. Some pupils developed the idea that flowers appear to die in Winter, then reappear in Spring with new life. Others wrote poems, some in specific shapes, like 'Easter-wings', to reinforce the meaning of their verse.

One Year 4 entrant commented 'It was interesting learning about George Herbert because he was vicar of Bemerton a long time ago'. 'We made cards with flowers on,' said another, 'which was fun. George Herbert wrote a poem about flowers dying and coming back to life again.'

Attracting an impressive number of entrants, the competition drew out a wonderful range of talent, and three prizes were awarded by Dori Rockefeller at a school assembly. The winners' work was later put on public display in Salisbury Library.

Above
Toby Scrase of Bemerton St John Primary School receiving his prize from Dori Rockefeller

'It was a fantastic morning. Before… I thought the poems were very difficult, but came away feeling that I understood something about Herbert. It gave me a taste of English at university…'

'It was such a treat to be able to listen to Rowan Williams – and then, in the plenary, to hear the students talking so insightfully about the poetry.'

Senior schools' event with Rowan Williams

In response to a request from Rowan to meet and work with young people during the Festival, a morning seminar on Herbert was hosted at Bishop Wordsworth's School on Friday, 11th July. Attended by Year 12 students from BWS and South Wilts Grammar School for Girls, the seminar began with an introductory talk from Rowan on Herbert's life and work. Students then broke into five groups, each of which read and discussed one of the following poems: 'A Wreath', 'Easter-wings', 'Paradise', 'The Altar' and 'The Church-floore'. Finally, the groups reconvened to present and comment on their poem.

The group studying 'Paradise' responded with some creative writing of their own. Taking 'order' as the focus of their discussion, students considered the way in which Herbert and the metaphysical poets might seek to communicate truths about the human condition through the medium of a conceit. The students then chose their own place of order or sanctuary and explored what might be learned there through an extended metaphor. 'There was a guide for each stanza,' explained a staff member, 'based on the essence of each of Herbert's verses in 'Paradise'. We then linked this exercise back to a close reading of 'Paradise' – picking out similar ideas and marvelling at how much better Herbert is at this poetry lark than we are!'

Afterwards, Rowan received a summary of the students' work at the event. He responded 'I was really delighted to have the material from the school. I thoroughly enjoyed being with you all, and this is the icing on the cake for me!'

Above
Rowan Williams speaking to senior students from Bishop Wordsworth's and South Wilts Grammar Schools

Picture courtesy of John Cox

'I really enjoyed reading poetry that I would not have read on my own.'

'The Country Parson'

**John Chandler &
Rev Simon Woodley**

Saturday, 12th July

St John's Church,
Bemerton

John Chandler is a historian who has studied and written about Salisbury for more than 30 years. Under the Hobnob Press imprint, he has also published many books about Wiltshire. In 2005 he researched the social history of Bemerton and Fugglestone in George Herbert's time. He was appointed editor of the Victoria County History for Gloucestershire in 2011.

Rev Simon Woodley was born in Northampton (home of John Clare) and grew up in Bedford (home of John Bunyan) before training as an architect in Liverpool and Birmingham. He was ordained in 2000 after studying theology at Cambridge University, and served his title at St Martin's in the Bullring, Birmingham. He became Rector of Bemerton in 2004.

In 1630, George Herbert became Rector of Fugglestone-cum-Bemerton. In 2004, Simon Woodley became Rector of Bemerton. Would either man recognise the day-to-day life of the other? During a lively conversation, John Chandler and Simon Woodley teased out the similarities and differences between Simon's work as the current Rector and George Herbert's seventeenth-century experience.

Church, parish and parishioners

Both men arrived in the parish at the age of 37. The parish had a similar geographical size and shape in 1630 as today. 'Like me, Herbert had a multiple-church parish,' Simon said. 'He had two and I have three. He looked to Wilton more... I look more to Salisbury.' But while George Herbert had about 200 parishioners, nearly all of whom attended church, Simon has 16,000, of whom that same number of 200 are regular church-goers.

Above
Simon Woodley explaining how his job as rector differs from that of his predecessor George Herbert

'I am in the middle of church renovation - very like Herbert!' (Simon Woodley)

The priest, then and now

Herbert's background was aristocratic and he had honed his intellectual skills at Cambridge University. He had been an MP and was well known in Court circles when he asked for the modest living of Fugglestone-cum-Bemerton.

Simon came from a less privileged background but also went to university before spending time as a youth worker in London. He later went to Cambridge, like Herbert, where he studied for the priesthood. 'As for upbringing,' Simon observed 'Herbert was not like his parishioners at all. I think I'm lucky to be accepted by most people and am probably in the "middle".'

Unlike many of his contemporaries, Herbert made a point of getting to know his parishioners, visiting them in their homes and providing financial support when necessary. Today's parson has no private income, no patronage and can't realistically visit all 3000 homes personally. But Simon's support for his parishioners takes forms Herbert could not have envisaged, for instance welcoming the Trussell Trust into his church buildings.

Running the parish

Both men have to grapple with the administrative burden placed on them by their superiors and, in Simon's case, by other agencies. Both are and were leaders in Bemerton, representing their parishioners, providing impartial advice and coordinating the PCC and other church-orientated bodies: the committee trying to save St John's Church in Bemerton by turning it into a community centre is a prime example.

But as Simon commented afterwards 'It struck me that most of what I am doing – whether in community engagement, setting up a cafe, the Trussell Trust, or school work or saving St John's was barely begun in the first three years of my time here. So really Herbert hadn't scratched the surface when he died, and we never saw his potential.'

Left
John Chandler and Simon Woodley during their presentation in St John's Church, Bemerton

'[We discovered] so much more about George Herbert, poetry writing, and the wonders of different places around Salisbury.'

Above
Sculptor Jay Battle describing how he created his statue of George Herbert on the west front of Salisbury Cathedral

Walks in Herbert's Footsteps

Following routes that would have been familiar to George Herbert, two guided walks took place on Saturday 12th July, both ending in Lower Bemerton.

Salisbury to Lower Bemerton

'It was a pleasure and a privilege to lead the walk from below Jay Battle's fine sculpture of George Herbert on the Cathedral to Lower Bemerton, if not quite in GH's footsteps then certainly very near them,' recalls John Cox. 'The lovely weather, excellent company and shared enthusiasm were as evident on the walk as during the whole Festival.

'Among the walkers was Dr Hadrian Cook whose knowledge of the water meadows was kindly shown in an impromptu contribution as we paused on the Town Path and he considered the changes since Herbert's time. The reading I then gave of Herbert's poem 'The Water-Course' was enhanced by the committed choruses of the walkers in two groups asserting Herbert's unique double rhymes at the end of each stanza.

'After the reading of extracts from Walton at other stops, we arrived at the Rectory opposite St Andrew's where followed a triple delight for the walkers. Not only were we taken into the garden to see the more attractive seventeenth-century southern face of the building and its riverside setting, but the owner and writer Vikram Seth came out to greet us, and after his gracious welcome he eloquently read his poem 'Host'. Modelled on Herbert's 'Love (III)', it tells of his purchase of the building and his acceptance of the presence of the poet.

'Our final stop was at St John's Church to sing 'Teach me, my God and King' and to hear a reading of 'Love (III)', ending with its bidding to eat – appropriately directing us to our picnic lunch.'

'I loved the social events…, and met so many charming and interesting people.'

Wilton to Lower Bemerton

Led by Mark Wood, Rector of Wilton, the walk from the west of Salisbury passed through all three areas of George Herbert's parish of Fugglestone with Quidhampton and Bemerton.

As Mark reported, 'A diverse group (from 8–80+ years!) gathered in Herbert's parish church of St Peter, Fugglestone, and was treated to the first of a number of poetry readings that continued throughout the day. Then, replete with hi-viz jackets, the group made their way through the main gate into the grounds of Wilton House.

'After a brief comment on the literary circle gathered there by Lady Ann Clifford (second wife of the fourth Earl, Philip Herbert) who had arrived in 1630, the same year as Herbert, walkers received a "quiz sheet" of local and historical facts. At stopping points along the way, this was used to test the group's knowledge (and sense of humour!). Prompted both by these and by the beauty of our surroundings, conversations within the group were wide-ranging and thoroughly engaging.

'Within the grounds, we skirted round what would have been formal gardens in Herbert's day: there we liked to imagine he might have spent some time in contemplation. 'After a final stopping point by the "Daye House" (and a slightly "naughty" deviation into twentieth-century history, with discussion of Edith Olivier and Rex Whistler), we crossed the road into Quidhampton.

'From there a gentle but purposeful last leg took us along the quieter lanes to St John's School in Lower Bemerton. Here we were met by members of the Salisbury walk and we mingled conversationally during a well-earned picnic lunch.

'With fine weather and a friendly and talkative group, both current rectors of Fugglestone and Bemerton (Mark Wood and Simon Woodley) agreed that the walk had proved an enjoyable outdoor addition to the celebrations of their more famous predecessor!'

Above
*Walkers pause as they
cross the water meadows
for a reading from Izaak
Walton's The Life of
George Herbert*

Festival Committee

The George Herbert Festival 2014 was conceived by Canon Judy Rees, who chaired the Committee and who gathered together its members, with the aim of achieving a good cross-section of skills and representation across the venues and age groups. As Co-Chairman, Peter Webster was responsible for detailed organisation and coordination, with direct support from Secretary Lesley Burton and Administrator Pam Court. Financial management was in the hands of Joint Treasurers Charles Woodd, who dealt with all the transactions, and Chris Dragonetti, who oversaw the budget. Additional support was provided by Kate Weale and Rosemary Hawley.

Input from Bemerton was provided by the Rector Rev Simon Woodley and two members of his PCC, Linda Carley and Terri Seaton.

In addition, Bemerton events were overseen by Lis Woods, Chair of the George Herbert in Bemerton Group, and Eleanor Wordsworth of the Friends of St Andrew's Church. Wilton Rector Rev Mark Wood provided the link with his PCC and parishioners, and the liaison with Wilton House.

In Salisbury, support from Sarum College was coordinated by Linda Cooper and Jenny Brownhill with public relations support from Christine Nielsen-Craig. Liaison with Salisbury Cathedral was managed by the Precentor, Canon Tom Clammer.

The involvement of young people in the Festival was arranged and overseen by John Cox with the senior school students, and by Ivy Picton with the younger children.